Marketing Magic
Spells to Make Your Business
GROW

I0466844

Chris Balbi

DEDICATION

To every person who looks at social media and thinks,
I wish there was a magic spell to make this easier.

CONTENTS

THIS IS A BLANK PAGE - FOR **BOLD** IDEAS

There's a lot of empty space in this book… It's intentional, grab a pen, and when you read something you can 'make work' for your business.
Write it down!

1 YOU'RE GOING TO WANT TO FOLLOW @BOTOXBYMEESHA ON INSTAGRAM!

What a weird way to start a book, right? But did you give it thought, did you maybe reach for your phone, or maybe you actually followed through and did it…either way you're leading us to our first point in this book. People NEED to be guided! Before we get too deep into this guide, we should probably credential ourselves and let you know why you can trust us!

We're Meesha Aesthetics, a 5 Location MedSpa in Eastern Pennsylvania and we've got an 83% client retention rate (compared to the national average of 72%). We treat roughly 400 clients every day and somehow make each of them feel just as important as the person before and after them. Of course we didn't grow to this size overnight

CUE THE FLASHBACK:

The year is 2012 and Michelle Balbi is running as a solo Nurse Injector in a room tucked into an Endodontist office. She's got a business partner, Lisa, and an Esthetician,Liz, and the three of them are using a paper calendar to schedule clients via their personal cell phones. Lisa and Michelle started with just $500 in a joint bank account and a dream that cosmetic injectables could be 'less stuffy' than what was being offered in doctors' offices.

Nearly 6 months into their start, Michelle realized she couldn't be an injector AND scheduler at the same time so she enlisted the help of her son, Chris, who had a knack for customer service and, unbeknownst to her, a knack for marketing (which will come in handy later).

Chris began fielding calls and texts to schedule patients and truly began to learn the industry, it wasn't long before he saw an opportunity to provide

'Edu-Tainment' (educational entertainment) to clients in person before their treatments. Upon seeing that educated clients stuck around longer, and often purchased more (units of Tox, AND skin care…) a light bulb went off (what a tired analogy, but it fits). What if he could reach more people–and so @BotoxByMeesha on Instagram was born.

Instagram, a word we hear and don't even bat an eye at, it's so ingrained into our culture these days, but back in 2012, it was basically an app for sharing over filtered photos of food. Chris saw an opportunity to 'stop the scroll' (a literal full chapter on that later) by infusing a new type of content into the newsfeed: Edutainment!

Fast forward to 2024, @BotoxByMeesha has over 28,000 followers, all of which were organically grown, and are all 'real people' who take the time to engage in real content. No like farms or bots here! After all, what's the point of having 100k followers, if 90% of them will never benefit from what you're offering?

We're literally giving you the 'spells' you can use to accomplish the same thing (after all, we believe in community - not competition) - every chapter has a

✏ Spell - aka an action item you can do to Grow!

While this 'spell' book is primarily geared towards instagram growth, you can take the same framework and apply it to Tiktok or Facebook - we've used the same spells and garnished 72,000 followers on TikTok and 10,000 Followers on Facebook

Our Instagram hasn't just become a hub for clients, it's become a hub for other MedSpas to swipe ideas and use them for their own spaces - and WE LOVE THAT. We're all about community over competition, we all succeed if we all commit to offering honesty, safety and care to our clients.

Instagram has helped us fill our books, transform our one room office into 5 locations, 20+ providers and 20+ support staff, and we're going to explain to you, chapter by chapter, just how we did it.

So we ask again, do you want to grab that phone and give @BotoxByMeesha a follow? We promise you'll find useful information, or at least get a good laugh out of us, and we're down for either!

1.5 THE CONTRACT

Before we get started we need you to consider something - THIS TAKES WORK. You can't just read this book, try what you've learned for a week, and stop or give up if it 'doesn't work.'

I've trained 150 offices over the last 10 years, and the most successful ones, are those that gave it the good old college try for at least 3 months, after that, it become second nature and dareIi say, 'easy.'

BEFORE WE EMBARK ON THIS JOURNEY, I want you to make an agreement with me, and yourself, repeat after me...

I (say your name) am ready to make marketing magic happen. I'm going to read this book and then commit to trying something new for at least 3 months. And if I can't, I'll find someone in my office who can read this book, and get them to do it with / for me.

_____
(sign your name, unless this is a
digital copy, then you can just pretend)

But also, add the 'date' so you can look back to the day you started making 'progress'

2 ACCRUING AN AUDIENCE

Isn't it wonky how Kim Kardashian can name drop a product (usually one she's invested in) and it can sell out in less than 24 hours? It's thanks to her audience/following, she has X on Instagram alone so when she talks, X are listening. This is crucial to your success; it's why we're making this Chapter One. Even if you have an amazing service or message, if no one is there to hear it, does it even matter?

Cool story, so you're on board, you understand that building an audience is important, but how are you going to go about doing it? CEG - Continuity, Engagement, Gamification. These are your keys to success in building an audience - heck each of these gets it's own chapter later in the book, but here's the SparkNotes version:

Continuity - If you're not willing to work at building an audience, for literally just 45 minutes a day - put the book down (no refunds!) Don't keep going until you're going to commit to building an audience for at least 45 days, at 45 minutes a day. That's 33 hours, or one season of Grey's Anatomy…You've binged a TV show before, if you've got time to do that, you've got time to do this.

Building an audience is very much a snowball effect, the longer you keep the ball rolling, the bigger it will get, but if you stop, and let the snowball melt, it's hard to restart! There will be days you want to quit, days when nobody likes your post, but that's not the end of the world. We are goldfish (well, humans with goldfish brains when on social media); we won't remember yesterday's post tanked, but we'll be excited that today's post did well!

For years we trained MedSpas in person and the number one reason they failed, is they didn't see success in week one so they never posted in week two…and without that consistency, they never bloomed.

Engagement - I'm not talking about the kind to your fiancé, I'm talking about how you will interact with local businesses around you. Growing an audience is just as much about creating content as it is about consuming it. Go to your Instagram and search your local town's/city's hashtag - find other businesses (in or out of your niche) posting - and like/comment on their posts. Not only will that business be thrilled to get some likes/comments - but when Betty Boo who's looking for Botox sees @BotoxByMeesha commenting on her favorite restaurant's latest post about Raspberry Martini's - she's going to click that comment and see who @Botoxbymeesha is and hopefully give that page a follow too! BONUS this counts towards your 45 minutes a day, AND will give you a list of new restaurants, coffee shops, and stores to visit in your own town!

The Spell: Gamification - This is literally the next chapter, but here's your appetizer: Turn your posts into a game. Use words like 'I bet you can't guess how many laser treatments this took' or 'First person to tell us correctly which neurotoxin we used on this patient wins' - People love to 'win'- and you'll see your comments pile up quickly. Take this a step further by offering prizes - But where do you get these prizes? Keep Reading!

2.5 LEVERAGING THE LIST

Circle back to this section AFTER you finish the book, put these spells to WORK, and have a steady audience - having them 'on social media' is fun, but it's not going to 'make you money'.Honestly, I could write an entire separate book on turning your audience into customers, but the first step is here, for free, without having to procure the un-written sequel.

You've got to move your 'passive' audience who's just watching, into a more 'actionable' state by getting them to hand over their cell number or email so you can add them to your email newsletter list, or to a list where you can text them about promotions or parties!

This can be achieved by offering rewards for people to people that sign up for your newsletter / rewards app for the first time. If you're not quite ready for newsletters, a simple Google Forms will work to start collecting names, email addresses and phone numbers so you can truly get in front of people

This will also come in handy when you read the last chapter!

3 GETTING GAMIFICATION

Gamification isn't just a buzzword; it's a powerful tool that can transform how your MedSpa engages with its audience. By integrating game-like elements such as giveaways into your marketing strategy, you not only foster engagement but also educate and convert potential clients. Let's explore how to effectively implement giveaways to boost your brand's presence and drive meaningful interactions.

Understanding Gamification

Gamification draws its roots from various traditions, from scouting badges to loyalty programs in retail. At its core, it involves applying game mechanics like points, rewards, and competition to non-game contexts—in this case, your MedSpa marketing efforts. This approach taps into human psychology, motivating participation and loyalty through achievable goals and incentives.

The Power of Giveaways

Giveaways are a prime example of gamification in action. They allow you to reward your audience while achieving specific marketing goals. Whether it's increasing brand awareness, educating about your services, or simply fostering goodwill, giveaways can be tailored to meet diverse objectives. Here's how to effectively structure a giveaway campaign:

1. **Define Your Goal:** Start by clarifying what you aim to achieve with the giveaway. Are you educating about a specific treatment, promoting a new service, or simply engaging your audience?
2. **Choose Your Prize:** Select a prize that aligns with your audience's interests and your business goals. It could be a popular skincare product, a free treatment session, or even a gift card for a local collaboration.

3. **Craft Compelling Imagery:** Visuals matter. Use high-quality images or graphics that showcase the prize and convey excitement. This helps in grabbing attention and generating interest.
4. **Define Entry Requirements:** Decide how participants can enter the giveaway. Common methods include liking the post, tagging friends, answering a question, or sharing their own experiences related to your services.
5. **Engagement is Key:** Encourage interaction beyond mere entries. Respond to comments, engage with participants' stories, and create a buzz around the giveaway. This builds community and increases the chances of your content being shared.
6. **Selecting a Winner:** Be transparent about how the winner will be chosen. Whether through a random draw or based on creativity, clarity here builds trust and encourages more participation.
7. **Announcement and Follow-up:** Once the giveaway period ends, announce the winner promptly. Follow up with all participants, thanking them for their engagement and inviting them to stay tuned for future opportunities.

Creative Examples and Strategies

- **Trivia Tuesdays:** Use themed trivia questions related to your services. For instance, ask about lesser-known uses of Botox beyond cosmetic enhancements.
- **Seasonal and Theme-based Giveaways:** Tie your giveaways to current events, holidays, or trends. For example, offer a winter skincare package or a summer-ready treatment discount.
- **Website Easter Eggs:** Hide incentives like "Golden Tickets" or exclusive offers on less-visited pages of your website. This drives traffic and introduces visitors to all your services.
  - *A real-world example* - we told our audience on social media - a pesky leprechaun hid a 'golden Botox' on our website somewhere…and if you could find it, you would be entered to win Botox, check out the numbers below, the day of the contest 777 people visited our website, a huge spike!

Legal and Practical Tips

- **Avoid 'Giveaway' Terminology:** Use creative alternatives like *Give*a*Way* to bypass automated filters that might flag your posts and or trigger 'bots' to enter your comments and try and trick your clients into handing over their personal info
- **Compliance:** Ensure your giveaways comply with local laws and platform rules to avoid issues with spam filters or legal repercussions.

Conclusion

✎ *SPELL*: Reach out to your favorite 'rep', that person who always swings by at the end of the quarter and asks you to make a purchase…and see if they've got samples they can slide your way AND/OR look on your shelves for a product close to, but not quite expired, and now get ready to give that away.

Make a post that highlights the benefits of the product, then ask your clients to participate in an action like following your page and commenting something helpful. When it comes time to randomly pick a winner, google 'free random name picker' and any time result will do!

4 CULTIVATING COMMUNITY

Think back to high school or college—why did you join a club? If I had to bet, it was because you wanted to feel a sense of community. As adults, that need for companionship and connection hasn't gone anywhere. We still crave it. What if you could provide that same sense of community for your clients?

On the surface, your business provides services, and it might feel like once your transaction or service is complete, your interaction with the client is over. But there's one word that might cause your stomach to drop: retention. How do you get that client to come back? By making them feel like part of your community. This is where your online presence becomes crucial.

Creating a digital community might be the most ethereal chapter in this entire book. It's going to be sticky and tricky, but here's the best part: You don't have to do most of the work! Once you identify and nurture a few key community leaders within your social group, they will take on much of the effort. These community leaders will begin commenting and posting their own journeys and create content that you can re-purpose and share!

Identifying and Encouraging Community Leaders

Community leaders are the individuals who engage the most with your content—they comment, share, and discuss. To cultivate this kind of repetitive engagement, you need to focus on repetitive encouragement. Respond to people's comments, acknowledge their contributions, and show genuine interest in their opinions. If you're not responding to people's engagement on your social posts, what's their motivation to continue?

Building a Sense of Community Through Content

As you begin to produce more regular content for your social channels and find your unique voice, remember that your goal is not just to build a brand but to create an 'army' of support for your business. This means fostering an environment where your audience feels valued and connected to both your brand and each other. Here's how to do it:

Share Authentic Stories

People relate more to actual clients than they do to the brand itself. Ask your fans to share their stories. Feature user-generated content that showcases how your services or products have positively impacted their lives. This not only provides relatable content for your audience but also validates their experiences, making them feel appreciated and heard.

One of the peels we offer is called the Enlighten Peel, after application you've got to rock an 'orange' face for 6-8 hours... we inform our clients they're joining an exclusive club of ladies who've all gone through this, and invite them to add their picture to our collage of other people taking care of their skin, they love it!

Host Interactive Events

Online events such as live Q&A sessions, webinars, or virtual meetups can significantly boost community engagement. These events allow for real-time interaction and give your audience a platform to voice their thoughts and questions. It's also an excellent opportunity to showcase your expertise and build trust.

Create Exclusive Spaces

Consider creating exclusive groups or forums for your most engaged followers. Platforms like Facebook Groups, Discord, or even a dedicated section on your website can serve as hubs where your community can gather, share experiences, and support one another. These spaces foster deeper connections and a stronger sense of belonging.

Consistency and Authenticity

Consistency is key in maintaining an engaged community. Regularly post content that resonates with your audience and maintain an authentic tone. People are drawn to genuine interactions, and authenticity will make your brand more relatable and trustworthy.

Leveraging Feedback

Your community is a treasure trove of feedback. Actively seek out and listen to their opinions and suggestions. This not only helps you improve your services but also makes your audience feel valued and integral to your brand's growth.

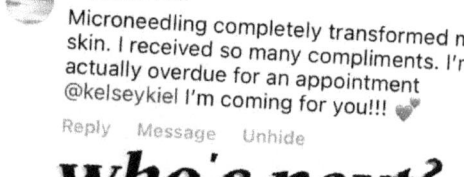

dap1028 14m

Microneedling completely transformed my skin. I received so many compliments. I'm actually overdue for an appointment @kelseykiel I'm coming for you!!! 🖤

Reply   Message   Unhide

who's next?

Recognizing and Rewarding Engagement

Recognize and reward the most active members of your community. Shoutouts, exclusive content, or even small rewards can go a long way in maintaining high levels of engagement. When people see that their participation is acknowledged and appreciated, they're more likely to stay involved and invite others to join.

Building a digital community is not a one-time effort but an ongoing process. It requires patience, consistency, and a genuine desire to connect with your audience. By fostering a sense of belonging and continuously engaging with your community, you can create a loyal base of supporters who not only return but also advocate for your brand. In the digital age, a strong community is one of the most valuable assets a business can have.

✎ **The Spell**: Post a photo of your favorite esthetician or stylist and ask something like 'Who's had Microneedling (or highlights, etc.) WITH US? Let's talk about it below!'

And if you end up with a 'I had a microneedling treatment, I didn't see change' comment, don't be afraid to step up and ask 'did you receive more than one as protocol dictates–sometimes we need a little more time to make magic happen'.

Remember community is built on honesty and transparency.

5 STOP SELLING

Before we dive deep into the intricacies, remember this formula: Education + Entertainment = EduTainment = Sales. Often, businesses focus solely on sales tactics, but the real magic happens when you invest your energy in educating and entertaining your audience.

The 70/20/10 Rule

Follow the 70/20/10 rule for content distribution on social media:

- **70% Education:** This forms the backbone of your content strategy. Educate your audience about your industry, procedures, products, or behind-the-scenes insights. Even mundane tasks like reconstituting

Botox or your cleaning protocols can be fascinating to your followers. These posts inform - and also build credibility and position your business as an authority in your field.

Example: "Did you know Botox arrives in a powder form and is reconstituted with Bacteriostatic Saline? At our clinic, we go through 30-40 bottles of Botox daily!"

•**20% Entertainment:** Keep your audience engaged with entertaining content that reflects your brand's personality. It doesn't always have to be dancing or elaborate stunts; it can be creative posts like photoshopping a famous book cover with a humorous twist, creating coloring pages of your staff, or sharing funny office pranks (always be kind!). This variety keeps your feed lively and relatable.

Example: "Settle an in office debate for us - are Marshmallow peeps yum or yuck?"

Why EduTainment Works

Educational and entertaining content serves a dual purpose: it captivates your audience's interest and builds a strong connection with them over time. By consistently offering value and entertainment, you create a reason for your audience to return to your social media channels regularly.

The 10%: Soft Selling with Heart

Finally, reserve 10% of your content for soft selling. This is where you subtly promote your services or products without overtly pushing sales. Avoid cliché stock photos with discount announcements. Instead, create genuine, engaging posts that resonate with your audience's needs and emotions.

Example: "We've got 4 different 'kinds' of Tox - and we want you to feel comfortable with any of them! Try two brands at the same visit (in 2 different locations) and get 10% off - Which brands have you already tried!?"

Why It Works: This approach feels authentic and personal, fostering trust and engagement. It's less about the hard sell and more about inviting your audience to participate in something special.

Embracing the EduTainment strategy on social media can transform your engagement levels and ultimately drive sales. By prioritizing education and entertainment while sprinkling in soft sales, you create a dynamic content mix that resonates with your audience and keeps them coming back for more.

Final Thought: "Remember, it's not just about what you post, but how you engage with your audience. Listen to their feedback, adapt your content strategy, and watch as EduTainment helps your business thrive in the digital age!"

/ **The Spell**: Cross compare a service you offer with something people can identify with - static vs. dynamic wrinkles on a forehead can be related to wrinkles in a dress - a wrinkle that only appears when you move is dynamic and can be treated with Botox (or starch) – whereas wrinkles that appear at rest, or on the dress while stationary are static and you'd need an iron, or microneedling to erase those - VISUALLY, this is as easy as wearing a dress to work and demonstrating the principles on video while talking about it.

6 NEWSJACK NOW

Before I dive in, let's just get the definition out of the way: Newsjacking is the art and science of injecting your ideas into a breaking news story and generating tons of media coverage and social media engagement. Bonus, this was Merriam Webster's Word of the Year in 2017!

Understanding Newsjacking

Newsjacking, at its core, involves leveraging popular movements or trending topics for your business's benefit. It's about capitalizing on the public's attention towards a particular event or phenomenon to amplify your brand's message and reach.

Examples of Successful Newsjacking:
•**The Ice Bucket Challenge:** A viral sensation that raised awareness and funds for ALS research.
•**The Mannequin Challenge:** Where groups of people froze in poses like mannequins, creating engaging videos shared across social media.

Recent Example: In summer 2023, the Barbie craze swept across social media and beyond. Burger King Brazil introduced a bright pink sauce for its Pink Burger, Joybird launched a Barbie-inspired line of fabrics and furniture, and fashion brands like Zara and Primark rolled out Barbie-themed fashion lines. These brands capitalized on Barbie's positive association to boost their own visibility. We jumped on board and used Barbie to host a one day 'grab the keys to barbies dream house' promo - it garnished us $500,000 in online sales!

Benefits of Newsjacking

Why engage in Newsjacking? When a popular movement or trend captures widespread attention, your business can ride the wave to gain exposure and positive association.

Brand Alignment and Positive Association

- **Positive Connotations:** Associating your brand with a positive trend or cultural phenomenon enhances its image.
- **Increased Visibility:** Leverage ongoing conversations to reach a broader audience and gain media coverage.

Example Strategy: "If a major film like Barbie receives substantial advertising, aligning your brand with its positive connotations can enhance your brand's reputation and visibility."

Considerations in Newsjacking

While Newsjacking can be powerful, it's crucial to ensure the trend or event aligns positively with your brand values and avoids controversy.

Mitigating Risks

- **Reputation Management:** Avoid associating with trends or events that may have negative connotations or could alienate your audience.
- **Cultural Sensitivity:** Be mindful of cultural or social contexts when participating in trending conversations.

Recent Example: "The 2024 Met Gala sparked widespread online discussion about celebrity disconnect. While discussing the event may not lead to cancellation, taking a strong stance could polarize opinions."

Conclusion: Harnessing Newsjacking for Your Business

In conclusion, Newsjacking can be a potent tool for enhancing brand visibility and engagement by aligning with current trends and events. By strategically participating in positive movements and staying mindful of your brand's image, you can effectively amplify your message and connect with a wider audience.

"Next time a viral craze or major event captures public attention, consider how your business can creatively and positively participate. Ride the wave to elevate your brand's presence and foster meaningful connections with your audience!"

/ **The Spell**: Grab a local paper (or visit USAtoday.com) or wherever you get your news from, search for the Entertamint section and start digging - new movies coming out? Award shows? Pop culture references? Did Justin Timberlake just get arrested? How can you tie that into your services to 'ride the wave'?

7 INFILTRATING INDUSTRIES
(THAT AREN'T YOURS!)

MedSpas, nail salons, hair studios, massage spaces, and even big retailers like Target all share a common audience. So, why not strategically 'sneak' your way into another industry to grab a new client or two? It's not just about infiltrating; it's about engaging with and supporting other local businesses. Here's how you can do it while being polite and mutually beneficial.

The Power of Engagement

Engagement is the key to building relationships with other businesses. Think about how excited you get when someone comments on your post. Be that person for another small business. Here's how to do it effectively:

Keep It Authentic

When commenting on another business's work, make sure your comments are genuine and specific. Instead of a generic "nice work," try something like "Wow, love that shade of blonde!" Authentic comments show that you're paying attention and truly appreciate their efforts.

Keep It Human

Avoid spamming a single account with comments, no matter how genuine they are. Commenting on every single post can come off as desperate. Instead, spread your comments across different posts and businesses to maintain a natural presence.

Keep It Local

Focus your engagement on local businesses. While it's nice to spread love across the country, engaging with local businesses using local hashtags will have a more direct impact on your business. It helps build a community around your physical location, leading to more relevant connections and potential clients.

Avoid Shady Tactics

Never comment on local competitors' posts with offers to try your services next time. This comes off as underhanded and can damage your reputation. Keep your comments positive and supportive without trying to steal clients directly.

Beyond Digital: Personal Touchpoints

Engagement doesn't end online. Take your efforts into the real world to make an even bigger impact.

Visit Local Beauty Spots

Grab a stack of business cards and visit local beauty spots in your area. Bonus points if you bring snacks! Introduce yourself, but keep it brief. Remember, you don't want to be a solicitor; you want to be a motivator and cheerleader. Show genuine interest in their business and offer your support.

Use HIPAA/Privacy to Your Advantage

A clever way to get a foot in the door is by leveraging HIPAA/privacy considerations. Bring cards and cookies to local businesses and say, "We wanted to thank you for all your referrals." This approach is both respectful and thoughtful, showing appreciation for their support without coming off as a salesperson. And who doesn't love cookies?

Building Mutually Beneficial Relationships

By engaging authentically and supporting other local businesses, you're not just building a client base—you're creating a network of mutual support. Here's how to further solidify these relationships:

Collaborate on Events

Consider hosting joint events or promotions with other local businesses. For example, a medspa and a hair salon could collaborate on a beauty day event, offering discounts to each other's clients. This not only attracts new clients but also strengthens community ties.

Share Resources and Expertise

Offer your expertise and resources to help other businesses. This could be as simple as sharing social media tips or collaborating on marketing campaigns. By helping each other, you create a supportive network that benefits everyone involved.

Recognize and Celebrate Achievements

Celebrate the successes of other local businesses. Whether it's a grand opening, a milestone anniversary, or a special achievement, acknowledging these moments fosters goodwill and strengthens relationships.

Expanding your client base by engaging with other local businesses is a strategic way to grow your presence and build a supportive community. By keeping your interactions authentic, human, and local, you can create genuine connections that benefit both your business and the community. Remember, it's not just about gaining clients; it's about building relationships that support and uplift each other. So, start engaging, both online and offline, and watch your network - and your business - thrive.

✎ **The Spell:** This is a two part spell, grab a wand and let's get cooking!

1. Google 'local bakeries' and find someone who does 'custom' cookies - ask if you can buy 12 'lip shaped' cookies individually wrapped

2. Visit VistaPrint.com and print the 'thanks for your referral cards' - see the template below

Now staple your cards to a cookie and go back to google and search 'local hair salons' or 'nail salons' or 'yoga studios' - anything that aligns with your brand - pop by, say hi, and give them a cookie + card combo - worst case you wasted $5 - best case you get a new client/follower!

8 OMNICHANNEL OPTIONS

It's a word worth 18 points in Scrabble, but for your company it's worth so much more. According to research, it takes 5-7 brand impressions to create awareness. If you're only advertising on social media, you're relying heavily on organic traffic. Even with some paid content, you'll still fight tooth and nail to get the necessary brand impressions to land a lead.

Enter Omnichannel Marketing. In its simplest terms, "omni" means "multi." So, we're talking about multi-channel marketing. This concept isn't new to you as a consumer. You've seen a billboard for Oreo, followed by a commercial for Oreo, then a tweet from Oreo, then Oreos in the grocery store, and Oreos on the cover of People magazine. All of these marketing efforts combined make you want an Oreo. In fact, I'm going to pause writing this book and go get myself some Oreos.

The Power of Omnichannel Marketing

Unlike Oreo, most businesses don't have massive marketing budgets. So, how can smaller businesses participate in omnichannel marketing? By using their lead/contact lists effectively and creatively deploying multiple marketing channels.

The Barbie Marketing Campaign: A Case Study

One of my proudest career moments was my Barbie Marketing Campaign. We offered 20% off online sales with the promo code "Dream House" for one day only. The campaign resulted in $500,000 in sales, and it wasn't just from one social media post.

For weeks leading up to the promo, we talked about it in the office and on social media. We placed physical Barbie boxes around our offices to generate buzz. On the day of the promo, we sent out text messages to our clients, distributed newsletters, and posted on social media. But it didn't stop there—we encouraged our community to post their "Barbie pink" outfits and tag us for giveaways focused on our "Dream House" promo. You couldn't look anywhere that day without seeing something about our promo.

How to Implement Omnichannel Marketing

Omnichannel marketing takes work and planning, but if no other office around you is doing it, your efforts will stand out and you'll "win." Here's how to get started:

1. Understand Your Audience

Know where your audience spends their time and tailor your channels accordingly. This might include social media platforms, email newsletters, text messaging, physical mail, in-office promotions, and more.

2. Develop a Cohesive Strategy

Create a unified message that will be shared across all channels. Ensure that each piece of content aligns with your overall campaign goals and branding. Consistency is key.

3. Utilize Multiple Channels
- **Social Media:** Use platforms like Facebook, Instagram, Twitter, and LinkedIn to reach different segments of your audience.
- **Email Marketing:** Send out newsletters and special promotions to your email list.
- **Text Messaging:** Reach your customers directly through SMS for urgent or special offers.
- **In-Office Promotions:** Use physical displays and in-person interactions to reinforce your campaign.
- **Collaborations and Partnerships:** Partner with other local businesses or influencers to expand your reach.

4. Engage Your Community

Encourage your community to participate and share their experiences. User-generated content can significantly amplify your campaign. For instance, during the Barbie campaign, we asked our community to post their "Barbie pink" outfits and tag us, creating a ripple effect of engagement.

5. Measure and Adjust

Track the performance of each channel and adjust your strategy as needed. Use analytics to understand which channels are most effective and why.

Benefits of Omnichannel Marketing

- **Increased Brand Awareness:** Multiple touchpoints create more opportunities for potential customers to become aware of your brand.
- **Improved Customer Experience:** A seamless and consistent experience across channels builds trust and loyalty.
- **Higher Conversion Rates:** Engaging customers through multiple channels increases the likelihood of conversions.
- **Enhanced Engagement:** Interactive and diverse content keeps your audience engaged and invested in your brand.

Omnichannel marketing isn't just a strategy; it's a necessity in today's competitive market. While it requires effort and planning, the payoff is significant. By standing out through a well-executed omnichannel approach, you can create lasting impressions, foster deeper customer relationships, and ultimately drive more sales. So, start planning your omnichannel marketing campaign today and watch your business thrive.

The Spell: Get yourself an 8.5x11 piece of paper and draw a circle - now add the numbers 1 - 12 around the circle (okay, draw a clock...) Flip the paper over and write on the top 'The goal of my next marketing blast/promo is…." Under that write "the main message of my next marketing blast/promo is…" Now under that message draft four similar, but appropriately formatted pieces of content

1. Website page
2. A social Media Post
3. An email Newsletter
4. A 160 character text message

Now flip back over, and on your clock, write out what time you're going to 'push' each of these same message segments to your audience. We always suggest working from least intrusive to most intrusive. For example, a website update is something your clients have to actively seek out - whereas a text message is a strong notification and shouldn't be sent before 10am or after 7pm to respect you clients time!

9 LOW-HANGING LOVERS

Have you seen the term 'bo-curious'? It's a playful meme that circulates every so often, describing individuals who are intrigued by Botox but haven't booked a visit yet. I LOVE bo-curious people and you should too! These individuals represent the lowest of the low 'low hanging fruit.'

Identifying Low Hanging Fruit

Low hanging fruit refers to leads that are easy to grab and likely to convert into clients quickly. These are individuals who show interest in your services but may need a little nudge or incentive to take the next step.

Recognizing Potential Clients

- **Engagement Signals:** Regular participants in giveaways or interactive posts show genuine interest.
- **Event Attendees:** Individuals who attend your events or engage with your content consistently.

Example Approach: "Take note of individuals who consistently participate in your social media giveaways or attend your events. They are indicating interest in your services but may need encouragement to make a decision."

Nurturing Relationships Through Engagement

How do you foster them? ENGAGE! It's called social media for a reason - BE SOCIAL. Respond to their comments, engage with their stories, and reciprocate the energy they give you.

Building Connections

- **Active Participation:** Respond promptly to inquiries and comments to maintain engagement.
- **Personalized Interactions:** Tailor responses to reflect genuine interest in their needs and preferences.

Example Strategy: "Initiate conversations with event attendees who took the time to visit your booth or participate in your activities. Start by acknowledging their interest and offering additional information or personalized recommendations."

Educating and Encouraging

These 'low hanging fruits' are much easier to educate and encourage to try your services than someone completely unfamiliar with your brand.

Effective Engagement Strategies

- **Time-Sensitive Offers:** Use promotions with low risk and high reward to attract potential clients.
- **Incentives:** Offer discounts or bundled services to incentivize consultations and trials.

Example Promotion: "For instance, offer 50% off a skincare product if they come in for a consultation on Botox. This not only gets them through the door but also covers the cost of the product, making it a win-win opportunity."

Seizing Opportunities

Embracing 'bo-curious' clients and nurturing low hanging fruit' in your marketing strategy are essential for converting interest into action. By actively engaging, offering incentives, and providing personalized experiences, you can effectively guide potential clients through their decision-making process and foster long-term relationships.

Final Call to Action: "Next time you identify a bo-curious lead, remember to engage proactively and offer compelling incentives. They're already interested - it's up to you to make their journey to becoming a client as smooth and enjoyable as possible!"

The Spell: DON'T MAKE A NEW POST (breath of relief am I right?) - Scroll through old posts and find people who've commented - now respond to those comments with something like 'It's been a minute since we talked about 'microneedling' - did you have any questions we can answer? It can also look something like this...

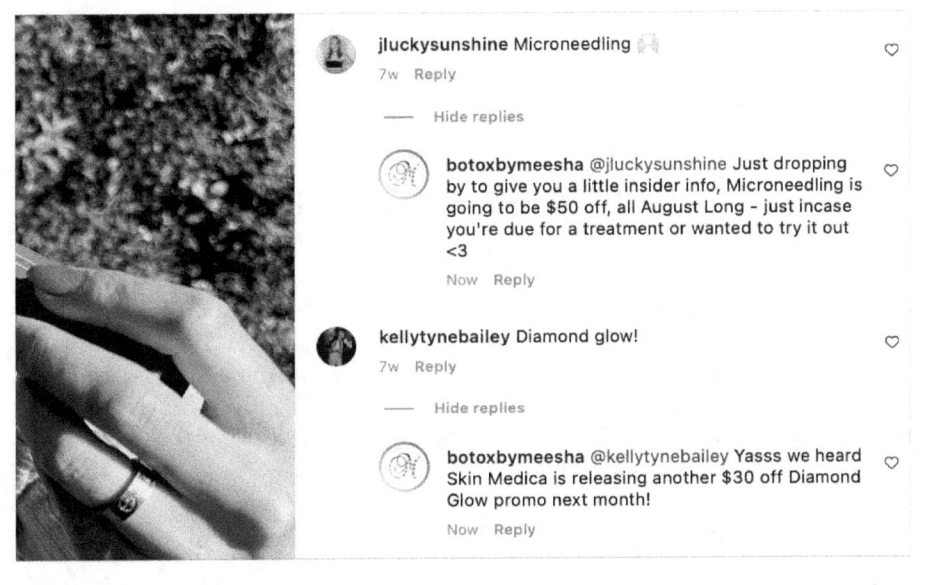

10 BENDING BACKWARDS

This is probably the chapter that doesn't fit into this book, but every spell book has a warning/guide that you should strongly consider. I would like to remind you that what you, we, I offer, are elective procedures. We like to pretend that Botox, or facials are essential to life, but at the end of the day, they're not. This means we've got to work harder than the company selling a life-saving drug, or water, or food, or other life essentials.

The Reality of Elective Procedures

In a crowded market filled with talented providers, it's essential to recognize that what we offer are elective procedures. Unlike essential products or services, these treatments are chosen by clients to enhance their lives, not sustain them.

Setting Yourself Apart

Exceptional Customer Service

- **Going the Extra Mile:** Bend over backwards for your clients to exceed their expectations.
- **Personalized Experiences:** Tailor promotions and services to individual client needs and preferences.

Example Scenario: "Imagine a loyal client missing a promo deadline by a few days. Instead of turning them away, honor the promotion as a gesture of goodwill. This not only retains their loyalty but also strengthens your reputation as a business that cares about client satisfaction."

Building Lasting Impressions

Clients will always remember two things... the businesses that 'screwed them over' and more importantly, the businesses that 'went above and beyond.' Between you and me, which would you rather be remembered for?

Cultivating Loyalty Through Exceptional Service
- **Personal Touch:** Acknowledge and reward client loyalty with personalized gestures.
- **Flexibility and Accommodation:** Accommodate special requests and situations whenever possible to enhance client satisfaction.

Example Strategy: "Consider creating personalized birthday promotions for long-time clients like Maria, who have shown unwavering loyalty. This not only surprises and delights them but also strengthens the bond between client and business."

Finding the Balance

Now a word of warning, find a happy balance between boundaries and bending backwards. It's crucial to maintain professional standards while striving to exceed client expectations.

Maintaining Boundaries
- **Consistency:** Ensure policies and procedures are fair and consistent for all clients.
- **Clear Communication:** Communicate clearly about what can and cannot be accommodated to manage expectations effectively.

"By prioritizing exceptional customer service and going above and beyond for your clients, you not only differentiate yourself in a competitive market but also build a reputation that attracts and retains loyal clientele. Remember, the small gestures often leave the biggest impressions."

/ *The Spell*: Can you run a sales report that tells you which clients 'spent' the most last year? Pick the top 5 and call them to personally thank them for keeping your lights on - okay don't say that, but perhaps a 'we love how much you loved us last year, we've got a gift set aside for you at your next visit' - and keep a cleanser or SPF set aside for them at their next visit

Can't run a report? Run out and grab 5 - $5 Starbucks gift cards, keep them in your desk, when you get that amazing client who had a rough day, hand one over and tell them to stop for some caffeine or a sweet treat on their way home...

11 PROMOS THAT PENETRATE

Raise your hand if you've heard this one:10% off Botox - now keep your hand up if you've heard of 14% off Botox?

First of all, if you're reading this at home, on a plane, or train and actually raised your hand, kudos for audience participation! Secondly, I bet you haven't heard of 14% off anything, and you're still thinking about who in the right mind would offer such an obscure number. Well, you are!

The Challenge of Traditional Promotions

In a world driven by value propositions, it seems like there's a flash promotion happening every week, on every webpage. Year after year, we've all been stuck in the same rut of traditional promotions, and consumers are starting to experience fatigue or what I like to call 'billboard syndrome' - that issue when after seeing the same billboard (or promo) consumers start to tune it out.

Combatting Consumer Fatigue

Thinking Outside the Box

- **Creative Concepts:** Introduce promotions that surprise and delight consumers.
- **Unique Offers:** Use unconventional discount percentages or tie promotions to memorable events.

Example Strategy: "Instead of the usual 10% off, consider offering 14% off for Valentine's Day on lip filler treatments. This not only stands out but also ties into a specific date, making it more memorable and engaging for your audience."

Promotions that Spark Conversations

Think outside the Box! I love a 14% off lip filler promo for 2/14 #ValentinesDay, or a '#TBT Prom Facial Promo' where we encourage clients to bring in photos from their prom and get 18% off while listening to 80s music.

These promotions start conversations, stand out and make consumers do a double take.

Engaging Consumers Creatively

Creating Memorable Experiences

- **Thematic Promotions:** Align promotions with nostalgic themes or current events.
- **Interactive Elements:** Incorporate interactive elements like music or photo-sharing to enhance customer experience.

Example Promotion: "Imagine hosting a 'Throwback Thursday Prom Facial Promo' where clients bring in their old prom photos, enjoy 18% off a facial, and groove to 80s music. This not only ties into nostalgia but also creates a fun and memorable experience that clients will want to share with others."

Standing Out in a Saturated Market

In today's competitive landscape, standing out is crucial to capturing consumer attention and driving engagement. By breaking away from traditional promotional strategies and embracing creativity, you can differentiate your brand and create lasting impressions in the minds of your audience.

We just 'slayed the day' but offering complimentary chemical peels (no peel peels) with every dermaplane in June - clients LOVED that they felt they were getting a 'free chemical peel' and it cost us $3/client and we saw an extra 110 clients in June!

Final Call to Action: "Next time you plan a promotion, think beyond the ordinary. Consider how you can surprise and engage your audience with unique offers and experiences that make them take notice. Break free from 'billboard syndrome' and start a conversation that resonates with your clients!"

✎ **The Spell:** This may be the hardest spell in the book because you've got to 'outsmart' me - your teacher - and think of a promo even I haven't thought of - okay, don't stress yourself out, but try and stand out among the offices around you.

What if you offered 5 free units of Botox to the first 5 people booked IF the 'Eagles' win the SuperBowl? Or IF Meryl Streep earns an Oscar?

Wouldn't it be unique if you gave 5 units of Botox (with the purchase of 20) to anyone who wore animal print to the office… sure to get people talking!

12 CHAOTIC CALENDARS

This entire chapter is one big spell or formula. I've trained nearly 200 offices now, and EVERY single one asks me, "Okay, yeah, but what am I going to post?" To solve this, I created a simple weekly calendar template to follow. This is just a guideline to get you started—every week can't be the same forever. You'll eventually need to talk about the Oscars, your receptionist's birthday, or trending topics. But when you're in a pinch, this is an easy "spell."

The Weekly Content Calendar

More Info Monday | Trivia Tuesday | Wayback Wednesday | Talkback Thursday | Feel Good Friday

Step 1: Pick a Topic

For this example, let's focus on Chemical Peels.

More Info Monday

Objective: Provide a comprehensive overview of the chosen topic.

What to Include:

- Detailed information about the chemical peels your MedSpa offers
- Different types of chemical peels (light, medium, deep)
- Benefits of each type of peel
- Potential downtime and aftercare
- Seasonal considerations (e.g. are they summer safe?)

Example Post: "Happy More Info Monday! Today, we're diving deep into the world of chemical peels. At [Your MedSpa], we offer a variety of chemical peels tailored to your skin's needs. Whether you're looking for a light refresh or a deeper rejuvenation, we've got you covered. Did you know that some peels require little to no downtime? Plus, we have options that are perfect for summer! Swipe left to learn more about our offerings and find the perfect peel for you. #MedSpa #ChemicalPeels #SkinCare"

Trivia Tuesday

Objective: Engage your audience with interactive content and gamification.

What to Include:

- A trivia question related to Monday's post
- An incentive, such as a free peel or a discount for the first correct answer

Example Post: "It's Trivia Tuesday! Time to test your knowledge. Can you answer this question about our chemical peels? 'Which type of chemical peel is best for minimal downtime?' Comment below with your answer, and the first correct response wins a free light chemical peel! Hint: The answer is in yesterday's post. #TriviaTuesday #WinWithUs #MedSpa"

Wayback Wednesday

Objective: Share historical or fun facts to educate and entertain your audience.

What to Include:

- Historical background on chemical peels
- Fun facts or anecdotes about the development and evolution of peels
- Any significant milestones in your med spa's history with peels

Example Post: "Wayback Wednesday is here! Did you know that chemical peels date back to ancient Egypt? Egyptians used natural acids like lemon juice to exfoliate their skin. Thankfully, we've come a long way since then! At [Your MedSpa], we use advanced, safe, and effective peels to rejuvenate your skin. Swipe left to see a timeline of how chemical peels have evolved. #WaybackWednesday #SkinHistory #MedSpa"

Talkback Thursday

Objective: Foster a two-way conversation with your clients.

What to Include:

- An invitation for clients to ask questions about chemical peels
- Prompts for clients to share their experiences or concerns
- Reassurance that their questions are valuable and will be addressed

Example Post: "Talkback Thursday is all about YOU! Have questions about chemical peels? Drop them in the comments below, and our experts will answer them. Remember, if you have a question, someone else might, too! Let's talk peels. #TalkbackThursday #ClientQuestions #MedSpa"

Feel Good Friday

Objective: End the week on a positive note with uplifting content.

What to Include:

- Before and after photos of clients who have had successful chemical peels (with permission)
- Testimonials or stories from satisfied clients
- Personal or fun content unrelated to peels, like pet photos or staff highlights

Example Post: "Feel Good Friday is here, and we have a fantastic before-and-after to share! Our lovely client, Sarah, achieved glowing skin with our medium-depth chemical peel. Swipe left to see her amazing transformation. Have a story to share? We'd love to hear it! #FeelGoodFriday #Transformation #ClientLove #MedSpa"

Planning Ahead

I often write out four weeks of content in advance so I can plan ahead. Eye-catching, often silly, costumes from Amazon (I do own an Egyptian headdress) make content creation more fun and engaging. To make planning easier, I google '[Month Year] printable calendar' and print it out to write my ideas. Some friends prefer digital tools, but I find paper planning more intuitive.

Tips for Planning:

- Use a calendar to plot out your posts
- Incorporate relevant holidays, events, and trending topics
- Stay flexible and ready to adapt your content based on audience engagement and feedback

Example Planning Process:

1. **Print a Monthly Calendar:** Google 'May 2025 printable calendar' and print it.
2. **Brainstorm Themes:** Jot down themes or special days (e.g., National Skin Care Awareness Month).
3. **Fill in the Blanks:** Assign specific topics to each day, ensuring a mix of educational, interactive, historical, conversational, and feel-good content.
4. **Prepare Visuals:** Plan and create necessary visuals, including photos, graphics, and videos.
5. **Review and Adjust:** Regularly review your content plan and adjust based on performance metrics and audience feedback.

By following this structured yet flexible approach, you'll have a robust social media presence that keeps your audience engaged and informed.

/ **The Spell:** Honestly, you should see this spell coming from a mile away - get a piece of paper, landscape and draw 4 lines vertically separating the page into 5 sections - Write Monday in section one, Tuesday in two, and so on...

Now plan out a week of content; you've got **this!**

Topic: Tox	Text	Picture Idea
MON	OMG! How much do you really know about everyones favorite neurotoxin - did you know it started out as a medical device for eye spasms... then..	A botox needle getting really close to the eye
TUE	Trivia Tuesday: What year was botox 'invented'	Sepia tone photo in a Victorian dress
WED		
THUR		
FRI		

13 F*CK FAKE FOLLOWERS

The Temptation of Fake Followers

So, you're thinking about boosting your Instagram followers with a quick purchase of fake accounts? Hold on just a minute! Sure, it might seem tempting to see that follower count shoot up overnight, but let's pump the brakes and talk about why that's a bad idea.

The Illusion of Fake Followers

First off, fake followers are just that – fake. They won't engage with your content, they won't buy your products or services, and they definitely won't help you grow a genuine community around your brand. It's like hosting a party and inviting a bunch of mannequins – sure, the room looks full, but is anyone actually having a good time?

Algorithm Smarts: Engagement Over Numbers

Secondly, Instagram's algorithm is smarter than you think. It values engagement over sheer numbers. If your posts aren't getting likes, comments, and shares from real people, Instagram will notice and your content will be pushed down in the feed. So, instead of reaching more people, you'll actually be reaching fewer.

The Ethics of Authenticity

Lastly, and most importantly, it's just plain dishonest. Building a brand should be about authenticity, trust, and creating real connections with your audience. Buying fake followers is like skipping to the last chapter of a book – you miss out on the journey, the growth, and the satisfaction of achieving something meaningful.

The Hidden Costs of Fake Followers

Damage to Credibility and Reputation

You might be thinking, "What's the harm? Everyone else is doing it, right?" Wrong! Buying fake followers not only hurts your credibility but can also damage your reputation in the long run. Imagine potential clients or collaborators discovering your inflated follower count – it could raise eyebrows and questions about your honesty and integrity.

Impact on Engagement Rate

Moreover, fake followers can actually harm your engagement rate. Instagram's algorithm is designed to prioritize content that resonates with real people. If a large portion of your followers are inactive or fake accounts, your posts will receive fewer likes and comments, which in turn affects your visibility on the platform. It's a vicious cycle that can ultimately hinder your growth and reach.

Financial Waste

Let's also talk about the financial aspect. Buying fake followers is essentially throwing money down the drain. Instead of investing in genuine marketing strategies that could attract real, engaged followers who are interested in what you have to offer, you're wasting resources on empty numbers that provide no return on investment.

Ethical Implications: Trust and Transparency

In an era where consumers value transparency and authenticity, misleading your audience with fake followers is a step in the wrong direction. Building a successful brand is about building trust, and trust cannot be bought – it must be earned through genuine interactions, quality content, and a commitment to ethical practices.

The Path to Organic Growth

In conclusion, while it might be tempting to take a shortcut to Instagram fame, buying fake followers is a risky move that can have serious consequences. It's far better to focus on creating authentic, engaging content and building a community of real followers who genuinely care about your brand. Trust us, the results will be worth the effort!

Practical Tips for Organic Growth

1. **Create High-Quality Content:**
   - Invest in good photography and videography
   - Share valuable, informative, and entertaining content
2. **Engage with Your Audience:**
   - Respond to comments and messages

3. **Use Hashtags Strategically:**
    - Research relevant hashtags
    - Mix popular and niche hashtags to reach a wider audience
4. **Collaborate with Influencers and Brands:**
    - Partner with influencers in your industry
    - Collaborate with complementary brands for cross-promotion
5. **Run Contests and Giveaways:**
    - Encourage followers to tag friends and share your posts
    - Offer incentives for engagement and participation
6. **Utilize Instagram Stories and Reels:**
    - Share behind-the-scenes content and daily updates
    - Create short, engaging videos to capture attention
7. **Analyze and Adapt:**
    - Use Instagram Insights to track your performance
    - Adjust your strategy based on what works and what doesn't

By focusing on these strategies, you can build a strong, authentic Instagram presence that attracts and retains real followers. The journey might be longer, but the rewards will be far more fulfilling and sustainable.

✎ *The Spell*: This is purely verbal - look in the mirror and say to yourself "I solemnly swear, not to be tempted into buying fake followers".

14 STORIES THAT STICK

Why Telling Your Brand's Story on Social Media is Crucial

First and foremost, sharing your brand's story humanizes your business. In a digital world flooded with ads and promotions, authenticity stands out. By sharing the journey, values, and people behind your brand, you create a connection with your audience that goes beyond a transactional relationship. People don't just buy products or services; they buy stories and experiences. Your brand's story gives them something to relate to, making them more likely to engage with your content and become loyal customers.

Humanizing Your Brand

Creating Connections

- **Authenticity:** Sharing real stories about your brand's origins, challenges, and successes makes your brand more relatable.
- **Emotional Engagement:** Stories evoke emotions, making your audience feel more connected to your brand.

Example Post: "Ever wondered how [Your Brand] started? It all began in a small garage where our founder [Name] decided to follow their passion for [industry]. Through perseverance and a commitment to quality, we've grown into the brand you know and love today. #OurStory #BrandJourney"

Differentiating Your Brand

Storytelling allows you to differentiate your brand in a crowded marketplace. Let's face it, there are countless businesses out there offering similar products or services. What sets you apart? Your unique story! Whether it's the passion that drives you, the challenges you've overcome, or the values that guide you, your brand's story gives you a competitive edge by creating a distinct identity that resonates with your target audience.

Unique Identity
- **Brand Values:** Highlight what makes your brand unique.
- **Customer Loyalty:** A compelling story can turn one-time customers into lifelong advocates.

Example Post: "At [Your Brand], our mission is to [mission statement]. We believe in [core values], which is why every product is crafted with care and precision. Discover the story behind our commitment to excellence. #BrandValues #QualityCraftsmanship"

Building Trust and Credibility

Moreover, storytelling is a powerful tool for building trust and credibility. By being transparent about your brand's history, mission, and values, you demonstrate authenticity and integrity, which are key factors in establishing trust with your audience. In an age where consumers are increasingly skeptical of advertising and brand claims, being open and honest about who you are and what you stand for can make all the difference in gaining customer trust and loyalty.

Transparency and Integrity
- **Trust Building:** Openly share your brand's milestones, failures, and lessons learned.
- **Authenticity:** Be honest about your journey, showing both the highs and the lows.

Example Post: "We've faced many challenges along the way, but our dedication to [core mission] has kept us moving forward. Here's a look at some of the hurdles we've overcome and how they've shaped who we are today. #BrandJourney #Transparency"

Engagement and Community Building

Lastly, telling your brand's story on social media provides valuable opportunities for engagement and community building. Encouraging your audience to share their own stories, experiences, and feedback fosters a sense of community and belonging. It turns your followers into advocates and ambassadors for your brand, amplifying your reach and influence.

Fostering Community
- **User-Generated Content:** Encourage customers to share their experiences with your brand.
- **Interactive Posts:** Create posts that prompt your audience to share their stories.

Example Post: "What's your favorite memory with [Your Brand]? Share your story in the comments or tag us in your posts. We love hearing from our amazing community! #CustomerStories #CommunityLove"

The Importance of Employee Stories

But it's not just about your brand's story. It's also about the story of your employees.

Humanizing Your Brand Through Employees

Personal Connections

Highlighting the stories of your employees humanizes your brand and adds a personal touch that resonates with your audience. People connect with people, not just logos or products. By sharing the experiences, passions, and personalities of your team members, you create a more relatable and authentic brand image.

Example Post: "Meet [Employee Name], our [Employee Role]. When they're not [job-related activity], they love [personal hobby]. Learn more about their journey and what they bring to our team. #EmployeeSpotlight #TeamStories"

Demonstrating Value and Appreciation

Furthermore, showcasing your employees' stories demonstrates that you value and appreciate your team. It sends a positive message to both current and potential employees that your company is a great place to work, which can help with recruitment and retention efforts. It also builds a sense of pride and belonging among your staff, as they see their contributions and achievements being recognized and celebrated publicly.

Employee Morale

- **Recognition:** Publicly acknowledging employee contributions boosts morale.
- **Recruitment:** Attract top talent by showcasing your positive workplace culture.

Example Post: "We're proud to have such an incredible team! Today, we're spotlighting [Employee Name] who has been with us for [number] years and has made a huge impact in [specific area]. #EmployeeRecognition #GreatPlaceToWork"

Enhancing Credibility and Trust

In addition to humanizing your brand and boosting employee morale, sharing your employees' stories on social media can also enhance your brand's credibility and trustworthiness. When people see real employees talking about their experiences, skills, and roles within the company, it adds a layer of authenticity and transparency that can help build trust with your audience.

Authentic Representation

- **Real Experiences:** Share testimonials and stories from employees about their work and the company culture.
- **Transparency:** Showcase behind-the-scenes looks at daily operations.

Example Post: "Ever wondered what it's like to work at [Your Brand]? Our team members share their experiences and what makes our workplace special. #WorkLife #TeamTestimonials"

Showcasing Company Culture and Values

Lastly, sharing employee stories can help showcase your company culture and values. By highlighting the diverse backgrounds, talents, and perspectives of your team members, you can demonstrate the inclusive and supportive environment within your organization. This can attract like-minded customers and employees who share your values, fostering a strong and loyal community around your brand.

Cultural Showcase

- **Diversity and Inclusion:** Highlight diverse voices within your team.
- **Company Values:** Share stories that reflect your company's mission and values.

Example Post: "Our team is our biggest asset! We celebrate the diverse backgrounds and unique perspectives each member brings to [Your Brand]. Here's how we're fostering an inclusive and supportive environment. #DiversityAndInclusion #CompanyCulture"

Conclusion

In conclusion, storytelling is not just a marketing strategy; it's a powerful way to connect with your audience, differentiate your brand, build trust, and foster community. Embrace the power of storytelling by sharing both your brand's journey and the personal stories of your employees. This dual approach humanizes your brand, enhances credibility, and creates a deeper connection with your audience. So, don't underestimate the importance of telling your brand's story on social media. Embrace it, share it, and watch your brand thrive!

✎ **The Spell**: Grab your phone, and get out the 'notes' app (or anywhere you can throw out thoughts' - if you've got a 'voice to text' feature even better - Click the 'voice to text' button and just start rambling - pretend you're talking to a bestie or parent who just asked 'okay but how did YOU get here, to where you're sitting right now…Take me from your high school/college days until now.'

Read what you just wrote and pull out your story from it - treat yourself to a new headshot, or have your bestie take a cute picture of you and post it with the caption "My Story:…"

15 SOCIAL MEDIA IS DYING

It's weird to end this book with the sentence 'social media is dying' - I mean, don't panic, it's not going away forever, or permanently - but at the time of publication (2024) there's a shift to over-saturation of content creators. Everyone is an influencer, there's so many accounts and celebrities, your customers are now reverting into craving 'real' and personal interactions.

The Shift Towards Authentic Interactions

In today's digital age, where social media is flooded with content creators and influencers, the authenticity of personal interactions is becoming increasingly valuable. Amidst the sea of online profiles and advertisements, customers are longing for genuine connections and meaningful experiences.

Rediscovering In-Person Engagement

Events and Community Outreach

- **Local Events:** Consider participating in local community events such as street fairs, music festivals, and mommy-and-me gatherings.
- **Networking Opportunities:** Attend industry conferences, PTA meetings, and touch-a-truck events to network and build relationships face-to-face.

Example Strategy: "Instead of relying solely on online engagement, consider setting up booths at local events where you can interact directly with potential customers. Offer personalized experiences and engage in conversations that resonate with their needs and interests."

The Importance of Offline Networking

I'm not saying you wasted your time reading this book (could you even imagine) - you're always going to need a presence online. But if you're panicking and thinking *'but I'm much better in person…"* - good, prove it to me (and yourself) get out there and start networking.

Building Trust Through Personal Connections

- **Networking Effectively:** Showcase your expertise and build trust through face-to-face interactions.
- **Personalized Approach:** Tailor your messaging and offerings based on real-time feedback and conversations.

Example Approach: "Use offline networking opportunities to showcase your expertise and build personal connections. Engage in meaningful conversations and demonstrate how your services can solve real-world problems."

Amplifying Your Presence

It's no longer an 'if you build it they will come' situation. We're now in a 'once you build it, go tell everyone it's available' world - so start making some noise, I'll be listening.

Integrating Online and Offline Strategies

- **Cross-Promotion:** Leverage offline interactions to drive online engagement and vice versa.
- **Consistent Messaging:** Ensure your brand's voice and values resonate across all platforms, online and offline.

Example Integration: "After attending a local event, follow up with attendees on social media. Share highlights from the event, testimonials from participants, and encourage further engagement through online channels."

Conclusion: Embrace the Shift

In conclusion, while social media remains an essential tool for marketing and engagement, the shift towards over-saturation of content creators highlights the increasing value of real and personal interactions. By actively participating in local events, networking opportunities, and community engagements, you can differentiate your brand and build genuine connections that resonate with your audience.

Final Call to Action: "Take advantage of both online and offline strategies to amplify your brand's presence and connect with your audience on a deeper level. Embrace the shift towards authenticity and start making meaningful connections today!"

The Final Spell: Put your phone on do not disturb - Go outside - breathe long and deep - we may be 'changing' lives but we're not saving them. Don't let the pressure of your job turn you into the villain of this spell book. I promise you casting spells will be a lot easier when you're clear headed, focused, and enjoy the day.

ACKNOWLEDGMENTS

This book wouldn't have been possible without my bosses Lisa Silvaggio and Michelle Balbi (hey mom!) - they've given me a playground to explore and test my thoughts, theories and campaigns. A huge shout out to my Dad and Sister for listening to me talk about work endlessly on every car ride, it probably wasn't fun for you but it was a good time for me! My best friend of nearly 20 years Bethany Sloane, for reviewing the analytics of every campaign and validating my results. A huge virtual hug to Cassi Ettman for telling me 'you can do this' and pushing me to be more self-confident.

Thanks to my editor Jackie Frick for tolerating my inconsistent use of camel case and periods. My innovative designer Michael Rios for the beautiful cover art work and dealing with my incessant deadlines.

And finally, of course thanks to my husband for being my forever A/B testing buddy, listening to every one of my ideas, even the bad ones.

ABOUT THE AUTHOR

Chris lives in Philadelphia with his Husband and dog Maggie. He's no stranger to writing in the third person after spending his High School / College days writing biographies for his days spent in Theatre Programs before switching gears to start his career in digital marketing. Starting his career in higher Ed, moving to automotive and eventually landing in Aesthetics for the last 15 years, he finds a lot of joy both educating other medical spas, and reminding his clients that they're already beautiful.